A Let's-Read-and-Find-Out-Book™

Revised Edition

MY FIVE SENSES
by
ALIKI

SCHOLASTIC INC.

New York   Toronto   London   Auckland   Sydney
Mexico City   New Delhi   Hong Kong

ISBN 0-590-99449-2

Copyright © 1962, 1989 by Aliki Brandenberg.
All rights reserved. Published by Scholastic Inc.,
555 Broadway, New York, NY 10012,
by arrangement with HarperCollins Publishers.
SCHOLASTIC and associated logos are trademarks and/or registered
trademarks of Scholastic Inc.

36 35 34 33 32   13 14 15 16 17 18/0

Printed in the U.S.A.

The *Let's-Read-and-Find-Out Science Book* series was originated by Dr. Franklyn M. Branley, Astronomer Emeritus and former Chairman of the American Museum-Hayden Planetarium, and was formerly co-edited by him and Dr. Roma Gans, Professor Emeritus of Childhood Education, Teachers College, Columbia University.

MY FIVE SENSES

for my sister, Helen Lambros

I can see! I see with my eyes.

I can hear! I hear with my ears.

I can smell! I smell with my nose.

I can taste! I taste with my tongue.

I can touch! I touch with my fingers.

13

I do all this with my senses.

I have five senses.

When I see the sun or a frog

or my baby sister,

I use my sense of sight. I am seeing.

When I hear a drum or a fire engine
or a bird,
I use my sense of hearing.
I am hearing.

When I smell soap or a pine tree
or cookies just out of the oven,
I use my sense of smell.
I am smelling.

When I drink my milk
and eat my food,
I use my sense of taste.
I am tasting.

When I touch a kitten or a balloon or water,

I use my sense of touch.

I am touching.

Sometimes I use all my senses at once.

Sometimes I use only one.

I often play a game with myself.

I guess how many senses I am using at that time.

When I look at the moon and the stars,

I use one sense.

I am seeing.

When I laugh and play with my puppy,
I use four senses.
I see, hear, smell, and touch.

When I bounce a ball, I use three senses.

I see, hear, touch.

Sometimes I use more of one sense
and less of another.
But each sense is very important to me,
because it makes me aware.

To be aware is to see all there is to see...

hear all there is to hear...

smell all there is to smell...

taste all there is to taste...

touch all there is to touch.

Wherever I go, whatever I do,
every minute of the day,
my senses are working.

They make me aware.